EDGE
BOOKS

The Kids' Guide to

paper

AIRPLANES

by Christopher L. Harbo

745.592
j H

PARK
RIDGE
PUBLIC
LIBRARY

Capstone
press®

Mankato, Minnesota

Edge Books are published by Capstone Press,
151 Good Counsel Drive, P.O. Box 669, Mankato, Minnesota 56002.
www.capstonepress.com

Copyright © 2009 by Capstone Press, a Capstone Publishers company.
All rights reserved. No part of this publication may be reproduced in whole or in
part, or stored in a retrieval system, or transmitted in any form or by any means,
electronic, mechanical, photocopying, recording, or otherwise, without written
permission of the publisher.
For information regarding permission, write to Capstone Press,
151 Good Counsel Drive, P.O. Box 669, Dept. R, Mankato, Minnesota 56002.
Printed in the United States of America

Library of Congress Cataloging-in-Publication Data
Harbo, Christopher L.
   The kids' guide to paper airplanes / by Christopher L. Harbo.
   p. em. — (Edge books. Kids' guides)
   "Provides instructions and diagrams for making a variety of traditional paper
airplanes" —Provided by publisher.
   Includes bibliographical references and index.
   ISBN-13: 978-1-4296-2274-5 (hardcover)
   ISBN-10: 1-4296-2274-1 (hardcover)
   1. Paper airplanes — Juvenile literature. I. Title.
TL778.H37 2009
745.592 — dc22   2008029688

Editorial Credits

Bobbi J. Wyss, designer; Marcy Morin, project production

Photo Credits

Capstone Press/TJ Thoraldson Digital Photography, all

1 2 3 4 5 6 14 13 12 11 10 09

TABLE OF CONTENTS

Long before people flew real airplanes into the great blue yonder, they were tossing around paper planes. In fact, paper airplanes helped the great thinkers and scientists of old explore the science of flight. For most people, though, paper airplanes have always been a great way to have some fun.

If you want to fly, you'll need a good set of wings. Don't worry. This book doesn't involve flight training. You just need nimble fingers and a knack for folding paper. If you're up to the challenge, let's get started!

A Note About Materials

You won't be surprised that you'll need paper for the models in this book. Standard 8.5- by 11-inch (22- by 28-centimeter) notebook paper is easy to find and use. It also folds well and can be cut down to the size and shape needed for any model.

But don't be afraid to try out different types of paper. **Origami** paper works well for models that use a square. Origami paper is great for folding, and it's colorful. There's no rule that your paper airplanes need to be plain-old white. You can even try wrapping paper, scrapbook paper, or other bits of paper you can find lying around your house.

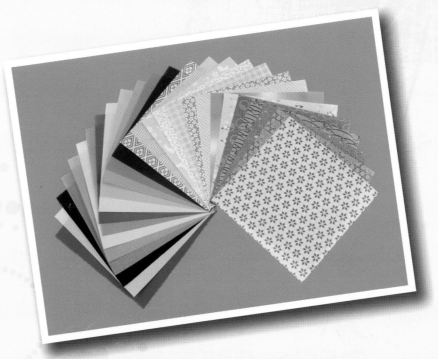

FOLDING TECHNIQUES AND TERMS

The instructions in this book use a variety of common folding techniques and terms. Review this list before folding the models. Then bookmark these pages so you can turn back to them for reference as you fold your planes.

Valley folds are represented by a dashed line. The paper is creased along the line as the top surface of the paper is folded against itself like a book.

6

Mountain folds are represented by a pink or white dashed and dotted line. The paper is creased along the line and folded behind.

Reverse folds are made by opening a pocket slightly and folding the model inside itself along existing creases.

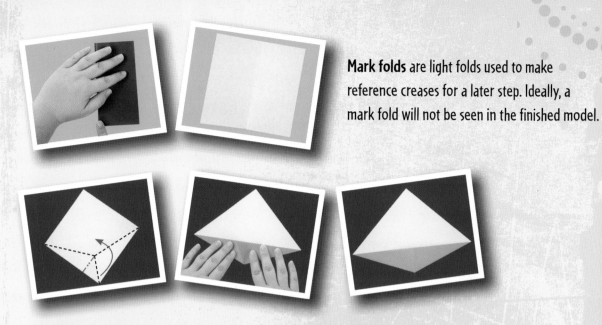

Mark folds are light folds used to make reference creases for a later step. Ideally, a mark fold will not be seen in the finished model.

Rabbit ear folds are formed by bringing two edges of a point together using existing creases. The new point is folded to one side.

Symbols and Terms

 Fold the paper in the direction of the arrow.

 Fold the paper and then unfold it.

 Fold the paper behind.

• • • • • • • • • • • • • • A fold or edge hidden under another layer of paper; also used as an imaginary extension of an existing line.

 Turn the paper over or rotate it to a new position.

CLASSIC DART

What You Need

★ 8.5- by 11-inch (22- by 28-centimeter) paper

Do you need to make a paper airplane quickly? Then the **classic** dart is definitely your plane. This model takes only about 30 seconds to make. In seven quick steps, you'll have it soaring across the room.

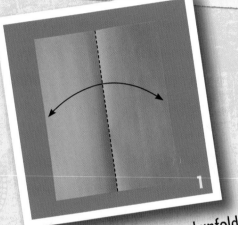

Step 1: Valley fold edge to edge and unfold.

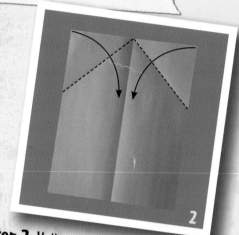

Step 2: Valley fold the corners to the center.

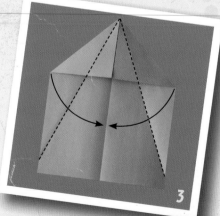

Step 3: Valley fold the edges to the center.

Impressiveness: ★★☆   **Complexity:** ★☆☆

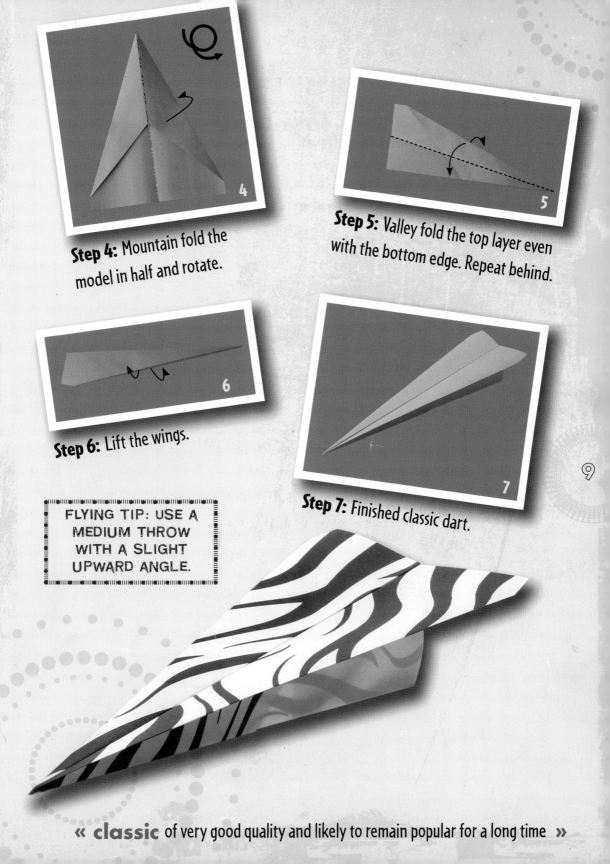

Step 4: Mountain fold the model in half and rotate.

Step 5: Valley fold the top layer even with the bottom edge. Repeat behind.

Step 6: Lift the wings.

Step 7: Finished classic dart.

FLYING TIP: USE A MEDIUM THROW WITH A SLIGHT UPWARD ANGLE.

9

« *classic* of very good quality and likely to remain popular for a long time »

SONIC DART

What You Need

★ 8.5- by 11-inch (22- by 28-centimeter) paper

The sonic dart gives the classic paper airplane model some style. With sleek lines and raised wing flaps, this plane looks **supersonic** with a gentle throw.

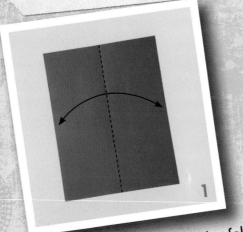

Step 1: Valley fold edge to edge and unfold.

Step 2: Valley fold the corners to the center.

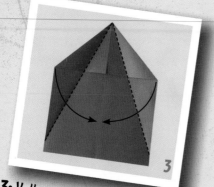

Step 3: Valley fold the edges to the center.

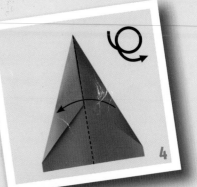

Step 4: Valley fold the model in half and rotate.

10

« **supersonic** faster than the speed of sound »

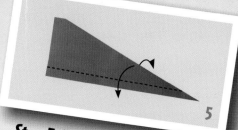

Step 5: Valley fold the top layer so the body of the plane is about 1 inch (2.5 centimeters) deep. Repeat behind.

Step 6: Valley fold the edge of the wing. Repeat behind.

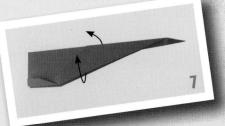

Step 7: Lift the wings.

Step 8: Lift the wing flaps so they stand up at 90-degree angles.

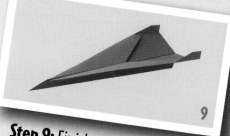

Step 9: Finished sonic dart.

FLYING TIP: USE A GENTLE TOSS WITH A SLIGHT UPWARD ANGLE.

Impressiveness: ★★☆   **Complexity:** ★☆☆

STEALTH GLIDER

What You Need

* ★ 6-inch (15-centimeter) square of paper

At first glance, the stealth **glider** looks almost too simple to fly well. But don't let this single-wing plane fool you. A series of folds puts much of the weight at the front of the glider. With the help of gravity, this glider flies amazingly fast.

Step 1: Valley fold edge to edge and unfold.

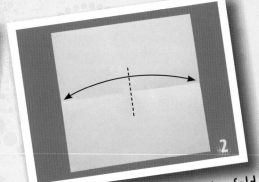

Step 2: Mark fold edge to edge and unfold.

Step 3: Valley fold the edge to the mark fold in step 2.

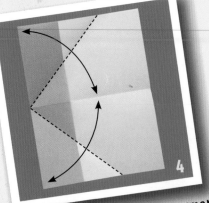

Step 4: Valley fold the corners to the center and unfold.

Impressiveness: ★★☆   **Complexity:** ★★☆

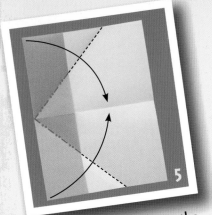

Step 5: Reverse fold on the creases formed in step 4.

Step 6: Valley fold the point.

Step 7: Valley fold the flaps and tuck them into the pockets of the point.

Step 8: Mountain fold the model in half and unfold.

Step 9: Finished stealth glider.

13

FLYING TIP: PINCH THE BACK END OF THE WING WITH YOUR INDEX FINGER AND THUMB. RELEASE WITH A GENTLE, FORWARD PUSH. THE HIGHER YOU HOLD IT AT LAUNCH, THE FURTHER IT WILL GLIDE.

« **glider** a lightweight aircraft that flies by floating and rising on air currents instead of by engine power »

SPACE RING

What You Need

* ★ 6-inch (15-centimeter) square of paper

Who said flying paper had to look like an airplane? Tell your friends that you can make a **circular** plane, and they probably won't believe you. They'll get a surprise when the space ring glides smoothly across the room.

14

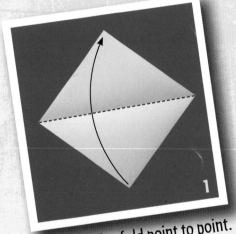

Step 1: Valley fold point to point.

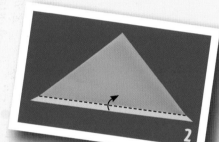

Step 2: Valley fold the edge to create a narrow strip.

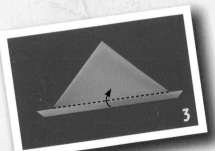

Step 3: Valley fold again.

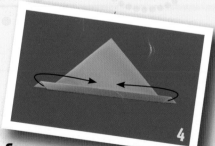

Step 4: Bend the model to bring the ends of the strip together.

« circular flat and round like a circle **»**

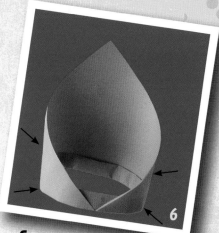

Step 5: Tuck one end of the strip inside the other as far as it will go.

Step 6: Shape the ring into a smooth circle.

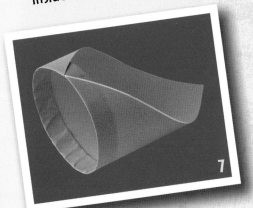

Step 7: Finished space ring.

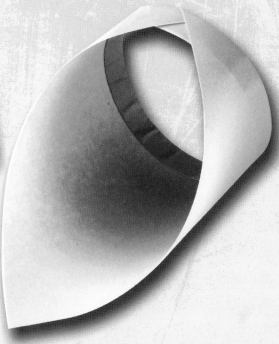

> FLYING TIP: HOLD THE POINTED END OF THE WING WITH YOUR INDEX FINGER AND THUMB. RELEASE THE SPACE RING WITH A GENTLE, FORWARD PUSH. HOLD IT HIGH WHEN YOU LAUNCH IT TO MAKE IT GLIDE FARTHER.

Impressiveness: ★ ★ ★   **Complexity:** ★ ☆ ☆

DOUBLE ARROW

What You Need
★ 6-inch (15-centimeter) square of paper

The double arrow gives the classic paper airplane a fun twist. As you finish folding, the plane gets its own built-in **cockpit**. When you launch this plane, imagine a tiny pilot at its controls.

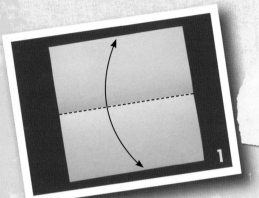

Step 1: Valley fold edge to edge and unfold.

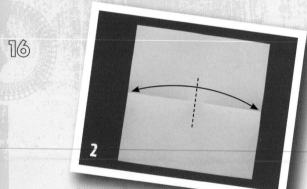

Step 2: Mark fold edge to edge and unfold.

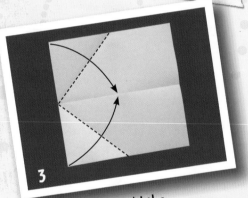

Step 3: Valley fold the corners to the center.

Step 4: Mountain fold the point to the mark made in step 2.

« **cockpit** the place where a pilot sits in a plane »

Step 5: Valley fold the edges to the center.

Step 6: Mountain fold the model in half.

Step 7: Valley fold the top layer even with the bottom edge. Repeat behind.

Step 9: Lift the wings.

Step 8: Pull up the triangle in the nose to form a cockpit.

Step 10: Finished double arrow.

FLYING TIP: USE A STRONG THROW WITH A SLIGHT UPWARD ANGLE.

Impressiveness: ★★☆   Complexity: ★★☆

HAMMERHEAD

What You Need

★ 8.5- by 11-inch (22- by 28-centimeter) paper

Do you want a good flier that can take a beating? Then look no further than the hammerhead. This blunt-nosed plane can handle the punishment of hitting a wall over and over again.

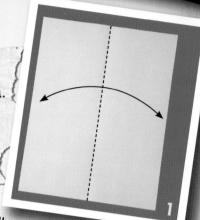

Step 1: Valley fold edge to edge and unfold.

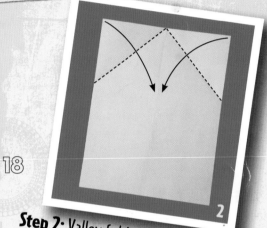

Step 2: Valley fold the corners to the center.

Step 3: Turn the paper over.

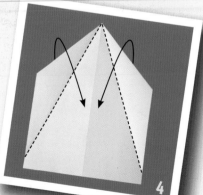

Step 4: Valley fold the edges to the center. Allow the flaps behind to release to the top.

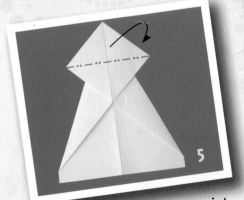

Step 5: Mountain fold the point.

Step 6: Valley fold the model in half and rotate.

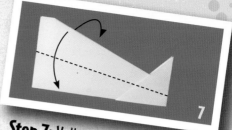

Step 7: Valley fold the top layer even with the bottom edge. Repeat behind.

Step 8: Lift the wings.

Step 9: Finished hammerhead.

FLYING TIP: USE A MEDIUM, LEVEL THROW. IF YOU CUT A NOTCH NEAR THE FRONT OF THE PLANE, IT CAN ALSO BE LAUNCHED WITH A RUBBER BAND.

Impressiveness: ★★☆ **Complexity:** ★★☆

SUPER PLANE

What You Need

★ 8.5- by 11-inch (22- by 28-centimeter) paper

If your school has a paper airplane contest, learn to fold the super plane. Of all the planes in this book, the super plane is one of the best for distance. This incredible plane can easily fly distances of more than 45 feet (14 meters).

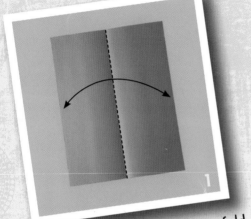

Step 1: Valley fold edge to edge and unfold.

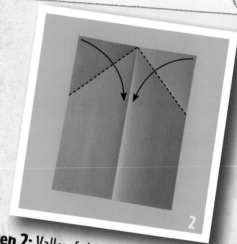

Step 2: Valley fold the corners to the center.

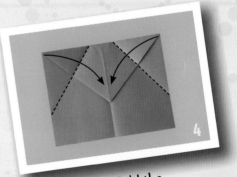

Step 3: Valley fold the point.

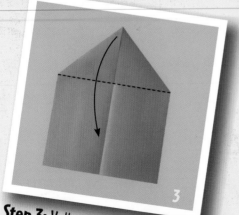

Step 4: Valley fold the corners to the center.

Impressiveness: ★★☆   **Complexity:** ★★☆

Step 5: Valley fold the point.

Step 6: Mountain fold the model in half and rotate.

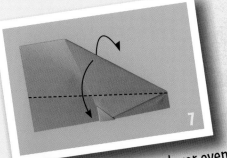

Step 7: Valley fold the top layer even with the bottom edge. Repeat behind.

Step 8: Lift the wings

21

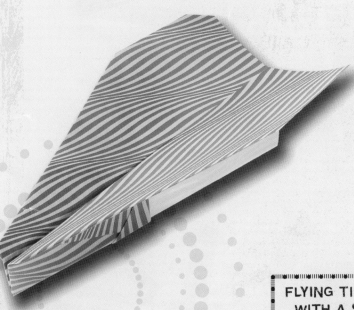

Step 9: Finished super plane.

FLYING TIP: USE A MEDIUM THROW WITH A SLIGHT UPWARD ANGLE.

ANGRY FINCH

What You Need

★ 6-inch (15-centimeter) square of paper

The angry finch seems to have a mind of its own. With a good throw, it swoops, dives, and carves wide curves in the air. Best of all, you'll never be quite sure where it will land.

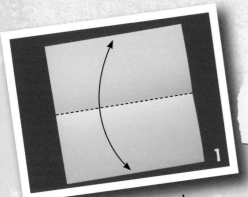

Step 1: Valley fold edge to edge and unfold.

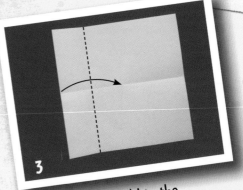

Step 3: Valley fold to the mark made in step 2.

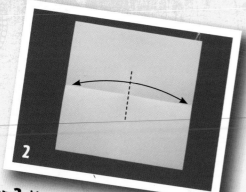

Step 2: Mark fold edge to edge and unfold.

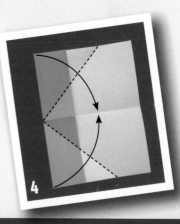

Step 4: Valley fold the corners to the center.

Impressiveness: ★★★   **Complexity:** ★★☆

Step 5: Valley fold the point.

Step 6: Valley fold the point.

Step 7: Mountain fold the model in half.

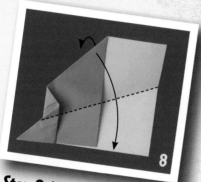

Step 8: Valley fold the top layer even with the bottom edge. Repeat behind.

Step 9: Lift the wings.

Step 10: Finished angry finch.

FLYING TIP: USE A STRONG THROW WITH A SLIGHT UPWARD ANGLE.

SILENT HUNTRESS

What You Need

* scissors
* 7- by 10.5-inch (18- by 27-centimeter) paper

Birds of **prey**, such as owls and hawks, swoop down silently to nab their prey. The silent huntress has a wide wingspan and a long tail. It glides just like a bird of prey going in for the kill.

Step 1: Cut a 2-inch (5-centimeter) strip off the end of the paper.

Step 2: Valley fold the strip edge to edge and unfold.

Step 3: Valley fold the corners of the strip to the center. Set aside.

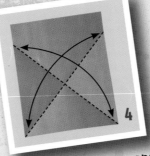

Step 4: Valley fold the large paper in both directions and unfold.

Step 5: Turn the paper over.

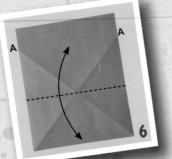

Step 6: Valley fold so the corners meet at A and unfold.

Step 7: Turn the paper over.

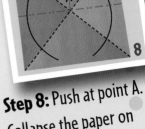

Step 8: Push at point A. Collapse the paper on the existing creases to form a triangle.

24

« **prey** an animal hunted by another animal for food »

Step 9: Valley fold the top layer to the point.

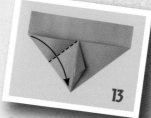

Step 10: Valley fold to the center and unfold.

Step 11: Valley fold to the center and unfold.

Step 12: Rabbit ear fold on the crease formed in steps 10 and 11.

Step 13: Repeat steps 9 through 12 on the left side.

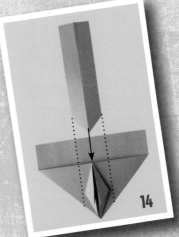

Step 14: Insert the strip between the layers so it fits in the point.

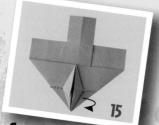

Step 15: Mountain fold the point.

Step 16: Mountain fold the model in half and rotate.

Step 17: Lower the wings.

Step 18: Finished silent huntress.

FLYING TIP: PINCH THE TRIANGLE BENEATH THE WINGS. RELEASE BY GIVING THE PLANE A GENTLE PUSH FORWARD.

Impressiveness: ★★★   **Complexity:** ★★★

What You Need

★ 8.5- by 11-inch (22- by 28-centimeter) paper

Depending on your throw, the raptor can be a glider or a stunt plane. Luckily, the plane's sturdy construction handles repeated flights like a pro.

Step 1: Valley fold edge to edge and unfold.

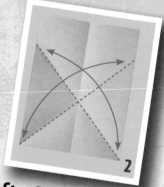

Step 2: Valley fold in both directions and unfold.

Step 3: Turn the paper over.

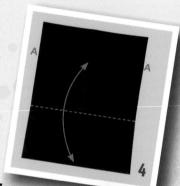

Step 4: Valley fold so the corners meet at A and unfold.

Step 5: Turn the paper over.

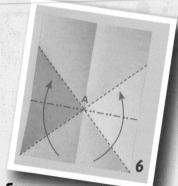

Step 6: Push at point A. Collapse the paper on the existing creases to form a triangle.

Step 7: Valley fold the top layer to the point.

26

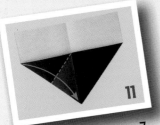

Step 8: Valley fold to the center and unfold.

Step 9: Valley fold to the center and unfold.

Step 10: Rabbit ear fold on the crease formed in steps 8 and 9.

Step 11: Repeat steps 7 through 10 on the left side.

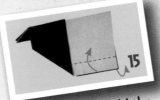

Step 12: Mountain fold the point.

Step 13: Valley fold the model in half and rotate.

Step 14: Valley fold the top layer. Repeat behind.

Step 15: Valley fold the top layer. Repeat behind.

Step 16: Lift the wings.

Step 17: Lift the wing flaps so they stand up at 90-degree angles.

Step 18: Finished raptor.

FLYING TIP: FOR A SMOOTH GLIDE, GIVE IT A MEDIUM, LEVEL THROW. FOR A STUNT PERFORMANCE, GIVE IT A HARD THROW WITH A STEEP UPWARD ANGLE.

Impressiveness: ★★★   **Complexity:** ★★★

J-ROM BOMBER

What You Need

★ 8.5- by 11-inch (22- by 28-centimeter) paper

The J-Rom bomber has a boxy look, but its flight path is straight and long. Once you've learned the folding steps, teach them to your friends. You'll have a blast challenging one another to see whose bomber flies the best.

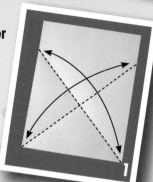

Step 1: Valley fold in both directions and unfold.

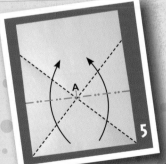

Step 2: Turn the paper over.

Step 3: Valley fold so the corners meet at A and unfold.

Step 4: Turn the paper over.

Step 5: Push at point A. Collapse the paper on the existing creases to form a triangle.

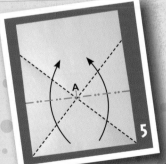

Step 6: Valley fold the top layer to the point.

Step 7: Valley fold to the center.

Step 8: Repeat steps 6 and 7 on the left side.

Step 9: Valley fold the point.

Step 10: Unfold the two flaps beneath the point.

Step 11: Tuck the flaps into the pockets of the point.

Step 12: Valley fold to the center.

Step 13: Valley fold to the edge.

Step 14: Valley fold to the edge.

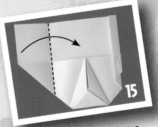

Step 15: Repeat steps 12 through 14 on the left side.

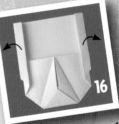

Step 16: Pull the edges of the wing out to create U-shaped channels.

29

Step 17: Finished J-Rom bomber.

FLYING TIP: PINCH THE PLANE ON THE TRIANGLE BENEATH THE WINGS. GIVE IT A MEDIUM, LEVEL THROW.

Impressiveness: ★★★   **Complexity:** ★★★

circular (SUHR-kyuh-luhr) — flat and round like a circle

classic (KLASS-ik) — of very good quality and likely to remain popular for a long time

cockpit (KOK-pit) — the place where a pilot sits in a plane

glider (GLYE-dur) — a lightweight aircraft that flies by floating and rising on air currents instead of by engine power

origami (or-uh-GAH-mee) — the Japanese art of paper folding

prey (PRAY) — an animal hunted by another animal for food

raptor (RAP-tur) — a bird of prey

supersonic (soo-pur-SON-ik) — faster than the speed of sound

Blackburn, Ken. *The World Record Paper Airplane Book.* New York: Workman, 2006.

Collins, John M. *The Gliding Flight: 20 Excellent Fold and Fly Paper Airplanes.* Berkeley, Calif.: Ten Speed Press, 2005.

Mitchell, David. *Paper Airplanes: How to Make Them and Fly Them.* New York: Sterling, 2005.

INTERNET SITES

FactHound offers a safe, fun way to find educator-approved Internet sites related to this book.

Here's what you do:

1. Visit *www.facthound.com*
2. Choose your grade level.
3. Begin your search.

This book's ID number is 9781429622745.

FactHound will fetch the best sites for you!

INDEX

ABOUT THE AUTHOR

Christopher L. Harbo loves origami. He began folding paper several years ago and hasn't quit since. In addition to paper airplanes, he folds paper into frogs, penguins, boxes, and stars. When he's not practicing origami, Christopher enjoys reading comic books and graphic novels.